From Seed to Sprout

Cultivating Long-Term Wealth Strategies

Andrew Galowey

Copyright © [Andrew Galowey] [2024]. All rights reserved. No part of this publication may be reproduced, distributed, or transmitted in any form or by any means, including photocopying, recording, or other electronic or mechanical methods, without the prior written permission of the publisher, except in the case of brief quotations embodied in critical reviews and certain other noncommercial uses permitted by copyright law.

Table Of Contents

Introduction

Chapter 1: Planting the Seed: Setting Financial Goals and Creating a Solid Foundation

Chapter 2: Selecting the Proper Soil: Understanding Investment Options and Asset Allocation

Chapter 3: Nurturing the Sprout: Developing Smart Investment Habits

Chapter 4: Seasonal Risk Management Strategies for Long-Term Success

Chapter 5: Blooming into Abundance: Harvesting the Benefits of Your Long-Term Strategy

Conclusion

Introduction

Have you ever desired financial security? Have you ever imagined a world in which you might follow your hobbies without being limited by finances? In "From Seed to Sprout: Cultivating Long-Term Wealth Strategies," we'll go on a journey together to make that ambition a reality.

This book is your personalized path to building money over time. We'll start by instilling financial awareness in you, guiding you to create clear objectives and lay a solid foundation. Then, we'll delve into the rich terrain of many investment possibilities, arming you with the knowledge to choose the best ones for your own circumstances. As your financial strategy starts to take shape, we'll encourage sound investing habits to guarantee consistent, healthy growth. We will not shy away from the inevitable storms that accompany every investing journey. You'll discover excellent risk management tactics to help you navigate market changes and achieve long-term success. Finally, we'll see your financial plan grow into wealth, allowing you to savor the benefits of your carefully developed approach. So, whether you're just getting started with your finances or want to improve your current strategy, "From Seed to Sprout" can help you create long-term prosperity and attain financial independence.

Chapter 1: Planting the Seed: Setting Financial Goals and Creating a Solid Foundation

Imagine a small seed resting in your palm. It has the potential for a beautiful bloom, a brilliant display of vitality and color. However, in order for that potential to be realized, healthy soil, nutritious water, and sunshine are required. Just like that seed, your financial future has enormous potential for development and stability. However, in order to build long-term wealth, a solid foundation is required.

This chapter will help you plant the seed of financial knowledge and create a solid foundation. We'll discuss the value of creating clear financial objectives, developing good financial habits, and building the basis for a secure future.

Why Set Financial Goals?

Many individuals go through life without a solid financial plan. They may fantasize about a comfortable retirement or a dream trip, but these fantasies remain just that until a specific strategy is in place to make them a reality. Setting financial goals is an effective technique for transforming ambitions into practical reality.

Consider your objectives as stepping stones. Short-term goals, such as saving for a down payment on a vehicle, serve as stepping stones to long-term objectives, such as financial independence. Here are some advantages of goal-setting:

- Increased Focus and Motivation: Defining your objectives gives you a clear path for making financial choices. Every dollar you make is a deliberate step toward realizing your ambitions.
- Prioritization and Budgeting: Setting goals naturally leads to prioritizing expenditure. You'll be able to deploy resources more effectively,

understanding which costs are beneficial to your aims and which may be cut.
- Increased Savings and Investment: Setting financial objectives motivates people to save and invest more. Seeing progress toward a certain goal may be very motivating, encouraging you to continuously invest dollars to your future.
- Improved Financial Literacy: As you establish financial objectives, you will naturally become more knowledgeable about financial products, investing techniques, and possible impediments. This continual study will help you gain financial understanding and prepare you for long-term success.

Goal-Setting Process: Charting Your Course

Setting financial goals involves more than simply wishful thinking. It requires careful preparation and a willingness to act. Here's a systematic strategy to help you get started:

- Identify Your Values: What is most important to you in life? Is it early retirement, the freedom to explore the globe, or ensuring your children's education? Aligning your objectives with your basic beliefs guarantees that you are working toward a future that reflects who you are.
- Brainstorm Your Goals: Let your imagination go wild! Dream big and write down all you want to accomplish financially. Don't be hesitant to set short, medium, and long-term objectives.
- Prioritize and categorize your objectives according to priority and timeline. Short-term objectives, such as vacation savings, may take priority over long-term ones, such as retirement preparation, in the early stages.

- Quantify Your Goals: Give each aim a clear, quantifiable target. This might be a monetary amount, a timeframe, or a particular milestone. For example, "Save $10,000 for a down payment on a car within 12 months" is a much more attainable objective than "buy a car."
- Create an Action Plan: How will you accomplish your goals? Break down each aim into tiny, manageable actions. Setting up recurring payments to a specific savings account, for example, may help you work toward your down payment on a regular basis.
- Review and revise: As your life changes, so should your financial objectives. Regularly assess your objectives, make adjustments as required, and celebrate your accomplishments along the way.

Building a Solid Foundation: The Essentials

Consider your financial foundation to be the rich soil on which your financial seed grows. Here are three essential factors for building a solid foundation:

- Building an Emergency Fund: Life may be unpredictable, and an emergency fund serves as a financial safety net. Experts suggest setting up 3-6 months of living costs to handle unforeseen occurrences such as job loss, medical expenditures, or automobile repairs. An emergency fund helps you to withstand these storms while without jeopardizing your long-term financial objectives.
- Managing Debt Wisely: Debt, especially high-interest debt, may be a substantial barrier to financial success. Prioritize paying off high-interest credit card debt. Consider debt consolidation tactics or refinancing alternatives to reduce

interest rates and better manage your debt.
- Creating a Budget and Tracking Your Spending: Understanding your income and spending is critical for making sound financial choices. Make a budget that categorizes your income and distributes monies for essentials, savings, and debt payback. Track your expenditure on a regular basis to verify you're sticking to your budget and identifying areas for possible savings.

Chapter 2: Selecting the Proper Soil: Understanding Investment Options and Asset Allocation

You've sown the seed of financial awareness, established your objectives, and laid a solid foundation. Now it's time to choose the appropriate soil - the investment vehicles that will nourish and allow your financial seed to grow. This chapter delves into the broad array of investing alternatives and introduces the notion of asset allocation, which is essential for risk management and optimizing development potential.

A Garden of Opportunities: Exploring Investment Options

The financial world provides a wide variety of possibilities, each with its own risk-reward profile. Here is a breakdown of some of the most popular investment vehicles:

- Stocks: Purchasing shares of a firm gives you a stake in its ownership and

future earnings. Stocks have the potential for huge gains, but they also involve more risk owing to market swings.
- Bonds: Essentially, you lend money to a firm or government in return for a fixed interest rate over a certain time period. Bonds provide a more secure and predictable income source, but they often provide smaller returns than equities.

Mutual funds are professionally managed investment vehicles that pool money from various participants and invest in a diverse portfolio of assets, such as stocks, bonds, or a mix of the two. Mutual funds provide a simple approach to get quick diversification while requiring lower investment minimums than purchasing individual equities or bonds.
- Exchange-Traded Funds (ETFs): Like mutual funds, ETFs are passively managed investment instruments that follow a specified index or market

sector. They have lower costs than actively managed mutual funds and give a transparent and cost-effective approach to diversify.

Real estate investing may be done either directly or via Real Estate Investment Trusts (REITs). Direct ownership has the potential for rental revenue and long-term value, but it needs substantial initial expenditure and regular care. REITs enable you to participate in a portfolio of real estate holdings without the complexities of direct ownership.

This is not an entire list; additional investing choices include commodities, option contracts, and private equity. However, for the majority of new and long-term investors, concentrating on a mix of the aforementioned possibilities offers a sound basis for a diversified portfolio.

- **The Power of Diversification: Introduction to Asset Allocation**

Consider planting only one variety of flower seed in your garden. While it may blossom brilliantly, it is vulnerable to illness or weather conditions, which might destroy your whole garden. Similarly, investing only in one asset class, such as equities, exposes your portfolio to substantial risk if that particular market sector suffers a decline.

Diversification is the key to risk reduction and long-term growth. Asset allocation is the act of separating your investing portfolio into several asset classes depending on your risk tolerance, investment objectives, and time horizon.

- Risk Tolerance: How comfortable are you with possible losses? Younger investors with a longer time horizon can often accept a greater risk profile and devote more of their portfolio to equities. As you near retirement, you may want to move your portfolio

toward more conservative investments, such as bonds, to emphasize capital preservation.
- Investment Goals: Are you saving for a short-term objective, such a down payment on a home, or a long-term goal, such as retirement? Short-term objectives may entail a more conservative asset allocation centered on liquidity and capital preservation. Long-term objectives might benefit from a stronger allocation to growth assets such as equities.
- Time Horizon: Simply stated, how long do you have before you need to retrieve your invested funds? The longer your investment horizon, the more time your portfolio has to recover from market swings. Investors with a longer time horizon can survive short-term market volatility while possibly benefiting from bigger stock returns.

Understanding your risk tolerance, investing objectives, and time horizon can help you identify the best asset allocation for your portfolio.

- **Building a Balanced Portfolio: Getting the Right Mix**

There is no one-size-fits-all method to asset allocation, however the following are some broad guidelines:

- Aggressive Investor (Long-term horizon, high risk tolerance): 70-80% stocks, 20-30% bonds, and cash equivalents.
- Moderate Investor (Medium Time Horizon and Moderate Risk Tolerance): 50-70% stocks, 30-50% bonds, and cash equivalents.
- Conservative Investor (short-term horizon, low risk tolerance): 20-50% stocks, 50-80% bonds, and cash equivalents.

Remember, these are just beginning points. The best asset allocation for you will be unique to your situation. To identify the appropriate allocation for your personal requirements, you must undertake study, understand the dangers, and, if necessary, speak with a financial counselor.

Chapter 3: Nurturing the Sprout: Developing Smart Investment Habits

Your financial seed has been planted on fertile ground, and your portfolio is taking form. Now comes the critical step of nurturing your financial sprout: creating wise investing habits that will guarantee its steady and healthy development over time. This chapter goes into essential strategies that can considerably increase your long-term financial success.

1: Embrace Regular Investing (Dollar Cost Averaging)

Imagine attempting to water your garden once a year. A single deluge may give immediate respite, but it is not a good plan for long-term development. Similarly, investing a large quantity of money at once might be dangerous since you are exposed to market swings at the moment of purchase.

Dollar-cost averaging (DCA) is an effective investment approach that entails investing a certain amount of money at regular periods, regardless of asset price. This strategy helps to average the cost per share across time, reducing the effect of market volatility. This is how it works.

Set up automated payments to invest a certain amount at regular times, such as biweekly or monthly. This assures steady contributions to your portfolio while also removing the emotional aspect of market timing.
- The power of compounding: Regular investments benefit from the magic of compound interest. As your assets increase, you will receive interest on both the original investment and the cumulative interest over time. The sooner you begin investing regularly, the longer compounding has to work its magic.

- Disciplined Approach: DCA eliminates the desire to invest huge quantities based on market highs or to avoid investing during market lows out of fear. Regular contributions promote discipline and guarantee that you remain invested throughout market cycles.

2: Befriend Mr. Compound Interest

Albert Einstein famously referred to compound interest as "the eighth wonder of the world." It is the mechanism by which your money generates interest on both the original investment and the interest accrued over time. The sooner you begin investing and the larger your time horizon, the higher the potential benefit of compound interest.

For example, suppose you begin investing $200 each month at the age of 25 and get an average yearly return of 7%. By the time you retire at 65, your total contributions will be $96,000. However, compound interest may make your portfolio worth more than $1 million!

Understanding the potential of compound interest emphasizes the need of beginning to invest early and regularly. Even tiny payments may accumulate into a substantial nest egg over time.

3: Control your emotions rather than allowing them to control you

Financial markets are fundamentally volatile. There will be moments of rapid expansion, followed by unavoidable adjustments. It is normal to feel emotions such as anxiety and exhilaration throughout these oscillations. However, allowing your emotions to guide your investing choices might be damaging to your long-term objectives.

Here are some strategies to help you control your emotions and keep focused on your long-term goals:

- Invest for the Long Term: Avoid being swept up in short-term market volatility. Concentrate on your long-term objectives and stick to a disciplined investing approach.
- Rebalance regularly: As market circumstances change, your asset allocation may deviate from your target percentages. Rebalance your portfolio on a regular basis to verify that it is still in line with your risk tolerance and investing objectives.
- Tune out the Noise: Do not base your financial choices on market froth or media hysteria. Stick to your research and investing strategy.

Remember that effective investment is a marathon, not a sprint. By regulating your emotions and staying focused on your long-term objectives, you can weather market storms and achieve financial success.

4: Stay informed while avoiding information overload

Financial knowledge is vital for making sound investing choices. However, it is critical to strike a balance between being informed and becoming overwhelmed by information overload.

Here are some tips for managing the information landscape:

- Identify Reliable Sources: Look for trustworthy financial materials, such as recognized investing websites, publications from renowned financial organizations, and books written by experienced financial specialists.
- Focus on the Fundamentals: Learn the fundamentals of investing, such as asset allocation, risk management, and diversification. Avoid getting mired down in sophisticated financial language or following trendy investing trends.

- Consult a Financial Advisor (Optional): For more tailored advice, consider working with a certified financial advisor who can help you create a customized investment strategy based on your individual requirements and risk tolerance.

By being educated about the financial environment while avoiding information overload, you'll be better able to make sensible investing choices that help you achieve your long-term financial objectives.

5: Review and revise as needed

Your financial condition, aspirations, and risk tolerance will change with time. Life throws curveballs, and your financial strategy must change appropriately. Make it a practice to assess your investing plan on a frequent basis and make any required modifications.

Here is a recommended timeframe for examining your portfolio:

At least once a year, perform a thorough assessment of your portfolio. Examine your asset allocation to verify it matches your current risk tolerance and investment objectives. Evaluate the performance of your individual investments. Consider adjusting your portfolio as required.
- Life Events: Major life events like as marriage, childbirth, career changes, or approaching retirement may all have a substantial influence on your financial requirements and objectives. Use these milestones to review your investing plan and make any adjustments to your portfolio.

These assessments are critical for ensuring that your investing strategy stays relevant to your changing circumstances and continues to move you toward your long-term financial goals.

Developing Smart Investment Habits for Long-term Success

By implementing the sensible investing practices recommended in this chapter, you'll be well on your way to sustaining the financial sprout you've planted. A effective long-term investment strategy is built around frequent investing, comprehending compound interest, controlling emotions, remaining educated, and revisiting your plan on a regular basis.

Remember that accumulating money is a journey, not a destination. There will be hurdles and failures on the road. However, by being disciplined, focused, and devoted to your strategy, you will grow that little financial seed into a blossoming garden of success, safeguarding your financial future and accomplishing your long-term financial objectives.

Chapter 4: Seasonal Risk Management Strategies for Long-Term Success

The financial journey, like a garden, has unique seasons. Periods of brightness and development are unavoidable, but so are storms and unpredictable weather. This chapter digs into risk management tactics to help you handle these unavoidable market volatility and ensure your financial strategy flourishes in all seasons.

Understanding Risk: Two Sides of the Coin

In the realm of investing, risk and profit are synonymous. High-risk investments have the potential for larger profits, while low-risk investments often provide lesser returns. Risk management is the act of recognizing, analyzing, and minimizing inherent hazards in order to safeguard your portfolio and meet long-term financial objectives.

Here are some of the important investing dangers you should consider:

- Market risk refers to the general volatility of the stock market. Stock prices may fluctuate owing to a variety of causes, including economic circumstances, interest rates, and geopolitical events.
- Interest Rate Risk: As interest rates increase, the value of existing bonds tends to decline. Investors expecting a consistent source of income from their bond holdings are at risk.
- Inflation Risk: Over time, inflation reduces the buying power of your money. Investments that do not keep up with inflation might reduce the value of your portfolio in the long term.
- Company-Specific Risk: Individual firms' financial health and performance may have a substantial influence on their stock prices. Diversification helps to reduce this risk.

Building a Resilient Portfolio: Diversification is Key

Diversification is the most effective risk-management method. This entails diversifying your assets across many asset types, including equities, bonds, real estate, and commodities. By not placing all of your eggs in one basket, you reduce the effect of a single asset class suffering a decline.

This is how diversity works:

- Reduces Portfolio Volatility: When one asset class declines, gains in another might help balance the losses. Diversification reduces the overall volatility of your portfolio.
- Reduces Concentration Risk: By diversifying your investments, you are less dependent on the success of a single firm or industrial sector.
- Long-Term Growth Potential: A diversified portfolio that includes growth asset classes such as equities

has the potential to provide better long-term returns.

While diversity is important, it is not a guaranteed method for avoiding all risk. However, by intelligently spreading your assets across asset classes depending on your risk tolerance and time horizon, you may greatly improve your portfolio's resistance to market volatility.

Understanding Risk Tolerance: Identifying Your Comfort Zone

Risk tolerance is the capacity to absorb probable losses in your investing portfolio. Knowing your risk tolerance is critical for making sound financial choices and devising an effective asset allocation plan.

Here are some elements to consider when evaluating your risk tolerance.

- Age: Younger investors have a longer time horizon and are more willing to

take on risk. As you approach retirement, you may wish to switch to a more conservative asset allocation to maximize capital preservation.
- Financial Objectives: Short-term investing objectives may need a more cautious strategy, but long-term goals may benefit from a larger allocation to growth-oriented assets.
- Financial Situation: Your overall financial stability matters. If you have a large emergency fund and other sources of income, you may be more willing to accept some risk in your portfolio.

Understanding your risk tolerance can help you choose asset allocation strategies that are appropriate for your comfort level and long-term financial objectives.

Beyond Diversification: More Risk Management Strategies

While diversity is an essential part of risk management, here are some more techniques to consider:

- Dollar-Cost Averaging (DCA): Investing a certain amount of money at regular times, as mentioned in Chapter 3, helps to average out the cost per share over time and reduces the effect of market volatility.
- Asset Rebalancing: As market circumstances change, your portfolio's asset allocation may deviate from your desired percentages. Periodic rebalancing ensures that your portfolio stays in line with your risk tolerance and investing objectives. This was also discussed in Chapter 3.
- Stop-Loss Orders: These are instructions to your broker to automatically sell an investment when it hits a preset price point, so limiting possible losses. However, they do not

promise a set price and may result in sales during brief downturns.

By combining these risk management measures with diversity, you may create a more robust portfolio that can weather the inevitable storms of the financial markets while remaining on course for long-term success.

Chapter 5: Blooming into Abundance: Harvesting the Benefits of Your Long-Term Strategy

The seeds you sowed in Chapter 1 have grown into a vibrant financial garden. Years of disciplined saving, wise investment, and managing market swings have gotten you closer to meeting your long-term financial objectives. This chapter delves into the benefits of a long-term financial planning approach and how to maintain your financial well-being throughout your life.

Reap the Benefits: The Fruits of Your Financial Labor

The benefits of a well-managed financial strategy go well beyond simply money building. It offers peace of mind, financial stability, and the flexibility to follow your interests. Here are some of the main advantages you may anticipate to get:

- Financial Independence: Consider a future in which you are no longer

dependent on a salary to satisfy your fundamental necessities. A successful long-term financial plan enables you to attain financial independence, or the capacity to live well without relying on a regular employment.
- Retirement Security: A well-funded retirement plan assures that you may live your preferred lifestyle once you leave the employment. You won't have to worry about living over your means or depending only on social security.
- Freedom to Pursue Your interests: Financial stability allows you to make life decisions based on your interests and goals. A strong financial foundation enables you to achieve your ambitions, whether they include touring the globe, establishing a company, or volunteering.
- Peace of Mind: Financial stability reduces a major cause of stress in our lives. Knowing you have a safety net in place gives you the courage to

confront unforeseen situations and live life to the fullest.
- Legacy Planning: A well-defined financial strategy enables you to leave a lasting legacy for your loved ones. You can protect your family's finances and help future generations.

These are just a few of the benefits that await you at the end of your long-term financial journey. However, achieving this level requires constant dedication and flexibility.

Life's Seasons: Changing Your Plans as You Grow

Your financial requirements and ambitions will change as you go through life. The financial plan you carefully constructed in your twenties may not be altogether appropriate for your fifties or beyond. The idea is to be flexible and tweak your strategy when your circumstances change.

Here are some important factors for adjusting your financial strategy during life:

Early in your career, prioritize creating an emergency fund, paying off school debts, and beginning to contribute to retirement funds. You may have a greater risk tolerance at this point.
- Starting a Family: Consider extra expenditures for child care and schooling. You may need to change your risk tolerance to a more cautious strategy.
- Mid-career: Increase your retirement contributions since your salary is anticipated to rise. Review your life insurance needs and think about college savings strategies for your children.

Prior to retirement, shift your asset portfolio to a more conservative mix to promote capital preservation. Review your retirement income sources and make any required changes.

- Retirement: Transfer your retirement assets to income-generating accounts to fund your preferred lifestyle. Continue to monitor your investments and make changes as necessary.

By evaluating your financial plan on a regular basis and updating it to your changing circumstances, you can guarantee that it continues to meet your requirements and steer you toward financial stability throughout your life.

Leaving a Legacy: Share Your Financial Wisdom

Financial awareness and preparation are strong tools for improving your own and your loved ones' lives. Consider sharing your financial expertise with others and assisting them in developing their own financial well-being. Here's how to leave a lasting financial legacy:

- Open Communication: Talk honestly about money with your family. Discuss

your financial objectives, strategy, and the value of financial stewardship.
- Financial Education: Give your children and loved ones the information and skills they need to make sound financial choices. Encourage children to adopt good money habits and begin preparing for the future as early as possible.
- Estate Planning: Create a detailed estate plan that specifies how your assets will be dispersed after your death. This may help reduce misunderstanding and dispute among your heirs.
- Charitable Giving: If you're enthusiastic about a certain cause, think considering including charitable giving into your financial strategy. Leaving a charitable legacy may have a long-term influence.

By instilling financial awareness and careful planning in your family, you may create a beneficial financial ripple effect for future generations.

Your financial journey is not a straight line with a clear end line. It's an ongoing process of learning, changing, and enjoying the benefits of your long-term investment.

Conclusion

You've finished this tutorial, but keep in mind that this is just the beginning of your financial journey. The seeds you sow now will grow into a future full of stability, independence, and the opportunity to follow your interests. But financial literacy is a lifetime endeavor, and what you've learned here is just the beginning.

Accept constant learning. As the financial environment changes, be interested and educated about new investing methods, tax legislation, and economic trends. There will always be more to learn, and ongoing learning will keep your financial plan current and successful throughout your life.

Adjust your strategy as life unfolds. Life is a journey with many unexpected twists and turns. A new career, a growing family, or a personal goal you've always wanted to pursue will all need changes to your financial strategy. Don't be hesitant to review your objectives, risk tolerance, and investing methods when your circumstances change. Remember that a great financial strategy is dynamic, not static.

Finally, share your financial knowledge with others. The information you've learned can have a significant impact on the lives of your loved ones. Talk openly about money with your family, encourage your children to develop healthy financial habits, and think about how you can leave a legacy of financial literacy and responsibility. Helping others cultivate their own financial well-being will result in a positive ripple effect that will last far beyond your lifetime.

So, go forth, armed with the knowledge and tools you've gained in "From Seed to Sprout." Plant your seeds of financial awareness, nurture them with discipline and smart planning, and watch your financial future bloom into an abundance garden. Remember that the path to financial independence begins with a single seed, and with dedication and perseverance, you can cultivate a future full of security and the freedom to pursue your dreams.